4 Tools To Use To Build A Website

Easily & Effortlessly

By Tina Young

4 TOOLS TO USE TO BUILD A WEBSITE
Easily & Effortlessly

Table of Contents

4 TOOLS TO USE TO BUILD A WEBSITE
Easily & Effortlessly

Is this book for you?

The person that would benefit from this book, is a novice and or beginner, familiar with the process of building websites; looking for good reliable tools to use, to get started.

4 TOOLS TO USE TO BUILD A WEBSITE
Easily & Effortlessly

Introduction

I've been designing and building websites for several years now and have used many of the basic tools needed, to build websites. Some tools were good and others not so good. I finally found the right combination of tools that help me design and build websites easily and effortlessly. This is what I would like to share with you.

This book will give you a nice head start to designing and building websites with ease. Sometimes having to do research on the basic tools used, to build websites, can cause you to delay getting started.

In this book I have answered all the basic tool questions for you, like...

- ✓ Where to register your domain name?
- ✓ What are some services that make a good web host?
- ✓ What content management system to use?
- ✓ What page builder is the easiest and simplest to use?
- ✓ What are some good plugins to install to add security to a website?

Let's get started!

Domain Name

You have probably seen the abbreviation DNS. This stands for Domain Name System. This domain name will be your address on the web. This is what people will type in, the address bar (www.yourwebsitename.com) to visit your website. So make it good and easy for people to remember.

CHOOSING DOMAIN NAME

First things first; coming up with a good domain name could be a job within itself. Most of the time common names are already taken. What I did was, jotted down three that I really liked. That way if my first choice was taken, I didn't have to try to think of another one, in the moment. The non-existing pressure that I would have put on myself would've kicked in and my mind probably would have went blank. Then I probably would have come up with and purchased a domain name that I really didn't put much thought, in to. I said all that to say come up with at least three domain names; that way you will have two more ready to go, if your first choice is already taken.

You don't even have to have a piece of paper handy to write your three domain names down. The next page was left blank, just for you.

	Brainstorming Domain Names

Step 1

Registering Domain Name

NameCheap is the first tool, out of the four that will be used to build a website easily and effortlessly.

They're many companies on the web where you can register a domain name. With that being said, I do have a bit of advice.... **Do not** register your domain name, with your web host. Reason being is if you decide to cancel your web host services for whatever reason and move your website to another web host you might run into some issues with your domain name. Because if your web host included a free domain name with hosting and you registered your domain name for free with that web host. The question becomes, who owns the domain name; if services are cancelled and or how much would it cost to keep ownership of the domain name?

Knowing what I know now, I would only use free domain name registration for testing purposes only.

DOMAIN NAME REGISTRATION

Three things that need to be done on NameCheaps website.

- ✓ Sign up for an account
- ✓ Do a search to see if domain name is available
- ✓ Register domain name

Go to www.namecheap.com.

Let's start with the first, *to do*, on the list, which is, *sign up for an account*. In order to register a domain name, you have to have an account. This account will be where you manage all your domain names.

As of the writing of this book, you can register a domain name with NameCheap for $10.98.

Quick Note

You can do a search on a domain name, without an account. But you will need an account to register a domain name.

Once you have your account you can do a search on your first domain name that you wrote down; by typing "yourdomainname.com" in the search bar (Fig 1-1), to see if it is available. I used the extension .com because this is what most people are familiar with. There are many different extension out there so choose what works best for you and or the business or organization you are building the website for.

Figure 1-1

When the search is completed you will see a check mark beside your domain name choice (Fig 1-2). This indicates that the domain name is available.

Fig 1-2

If the domain name is available, just click "Add to Cart" and continue on through the payment process; to complete the domain name registration.

If the domain name is not available you will see an "*X*" on the left hand side of the domain name and "*Taken*" on the right hand side of the domain name (Fig 1-3).

Fig 1-3

If the domain name that you chose is taken and you really just have to have that particular domain name, there's still hope! If you see a "Make Offer" (Fig 1-4) button, to the far right of the domain name, you can make an offer on that domain name by clicking the "Make Offer" button; which, once clicked, will allow you to type in your offer, for that domain name.

Fig 1-4

Quick Note

You have to renew your domain name every year.

ONE MORE THING

There's one more thing that you have to do with your domain name after it has been registered. You have to point your registered domain name to your web host nameservers.

After you had registered your domain name; you should have received an email from NameCheap. In this email NameCheap is letting you know, that your domain name is currently set to their default nameservers. I will go in to more detail, on how to change the default nameservers after we cover web host in *Step 2.*

Quick Tip

If you've already decided on a web host, you can point your domain name to your web host nameservers even before you sign up, with your web host.

QUIZ ME 1

1. What does DNS stand for?

    a. Domain Name Site

    b. Domain Name Service

    c. Domain Name System

2. You have to renew your domain name weekly?

    True

    False

3. You cannot point your domain name to the web host nameservers until you sign up with that web host?

    True

    False

Step 2

Web Host

The next step is to sign up for a web host.

A web host provides storage space for your website pages and allows access to your website, via your domain name which is also known as your url.

CHOOSING A WEB HOST

The type of services, that I look for, in a web host, surprisingly has nothing to do with the price.

I'm not sure if these services would be consider small in someone else's eyes but in my eyes these services are huge, in so many ways, for me. This is definitely because of some past experiences. Especially number four on the list. **Note: This list is not in any order of significance.**

Check out my four services from a web host, that are a must have, for me, below.

1. Free 1-click application auto installer- *This comes in handy when you want to install a Content Management System* (which we will cover in Step 3).

2. Free SSL

3. Free Automated Data backups

4. Malware Protection

Quick Note

These were the type of services I wanted, from a web host. The services that I listed may not be the services that are a must have, for you, from a web host.

SIGNING UP FOR A WEB HOST

I've used several web host in the past and I have learned a lot from each and every web host I've used.

The web host that is number one on my list and the one I recommend, is...... Drum roll please... Inmotion Hosting!

See Fig 2-1 for Inmotion Hostings comparison chart.

	inmotion hosting	HostGator	BlueHost	Arvixe	GoDaddy
✓ Ideal Less Than Ideal ✗ Unacceptable					
Solid-State Drives	✓	✗			✗
SSH & suPHP	✓	✓	✗	✓	✗
PHP, Ruby, Perl, MySQL, PostgreSQL, Python	✓	✗	✓	✓	✗
Max Speed Zones™	✓	✗	✗	✗	✗
Easy Google Apps Integration	✓	✗	✗	✗	✗
Free Automated Data Backups	✓			✓	
Free 1-Click Application Auto-Installer	✓			✓	✓
Better Business Bureau	A+	A+	A+	A+	A+
Customer Ratings (Positive/Negative)	+96/0	+63/-3	+18/-23	+2/-21	+42/-59
Money Back Guarantee	90 Days	45 Days	30 Days	60 Days	45 Days

Fig 2-1

Inmotion Hosting is the second tool we will be using.

Go to www.inmotionhosting.com. Once there, you will see that they're several different plans to choose from.

Click on the "*Learn More*" button under Business Hosting (Fig 2-2).

Figure 2-2

This will take you to the hosting plan page.

When you're just starting out, the *Launch* plan (Fig 2-3), is all you really need to get started. You can host 2 websites on this plan.

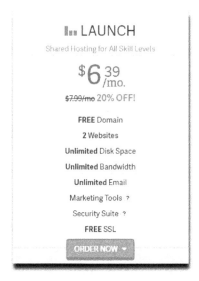

Figure 2-3

Hover your mouse over the "*Order Now*" button. You can select hosting for 1 year or 2 years.

The next part of this setup might be slightly different in some ways.

Websites are constantly being updated/modified. So the order of how things appear to you, may not be the same as how I have listed them in this book.

After you have selected your hosting plan, the next page is where you configure the server settings.

> ➤ The first section has to do with your *Server* (Data Center) location. Here you will just select what coast you're on.

> ➤ The next section on the *Configure Server* page; ask you "If you want a Dedicated IP". There should already be a tick by *'No Thanks'*.

> ➤ The next section is about your *Content Management System* (which we will be covering in Step 3). You can select to have it installed on your hosting account now or install it later. If you are following along with this book, don't install the Content Management System, at this time. I will be going in to more detail on how to do this, in Step 3, using the 1 click auto installer.

After you have configured your server settings, go ahead and click continue.

The next page is where you select a domain name, to host on your account.

> ➤ You have an option to purchase a new domain name or select one that you already own. After you make your selection click the continue button.

The next page is where you enter your email address.

> ➤ Enter your email address under *"New Customer"*. Make sure that this is a valid email address because the email address that you

enter, will be where all, your account information, is sent. Click the continue button.

The next page is where you enter your billing information.

➢ Enter your billing information and click the *"Review Order"* button.

The next page is where you review your order.

➢ Review your order. If everything is correct, continue on through, the payment process.

After you have completed the payment process, you will receive a couple of emails from Inmotion Hosting; one email will have the nameserver information. The other email will have a link to the AMP (Account Management Panel) log in page, where you will need to create a password, to log in to your AMP.

CREATING AMP PASSWORD

Time to open the email that has the link to create your AMP password. Once again this password will be used, to log you in to your AMP, where you can manage your domains and hosting plans.

Go ahead and click the link to create your password.

Make sure you write this password down; you're going to need it, in Step 3.

Nameservers

Okay, now that you have your domain name and a place to host your website; it's time to point your domain name, to Inmotion Hostings nameservers.

CHANGING DEFAULT NAMESERVERS

Log in to your Namecheap account. Once logged in, you can either click "Domain List" on the menu, on the left or click on "*Manage*" next to your domain name. Scroll down to "*NAMESERVERS*". The default nameservers will look something like [**ns1.defaultserver.com**], [**ns2.defaultserver.com**].

Next, open the email that has, the nameserver information.

Now change the default nameservers to Inmotion Hostings nameservers.

Make sure you change both nameservers and save the changes.

Okay, you're all set. Let's move on to the next step!

QUIZ ME 2

1. Why do you need a web host?

   a. To make google jealous.

   b. To store website pages.

   c. To secure website.

2. All web host provide free SSL

   True

   False

3. You can build an unlimited number of websites on Inmotion Hostings "Launch" plan?

   True

   False

Step 3

CMS and Themes

Now it's time to install the Content Management System (CMS) onto your web host account.

One of the most popular *Content Management Systems* out there, is Wordpress. Which is also the third tool that will be used.

As I said in *Step 2*, on "Web Host", one of the things that I was looking for, in a web host was "1 click application auto install". This is what will be used, to install the Content Management System (Wordpress).

If you decided to go with a different web host and that web host, does not, provide the 1 click auto install service, no need to worry; your web host, probably has some detailed instructions on how to install Wordpress, listed somewhere on their website. This book is only covering the additional information needed during the 1 click install of Wordpress.

INSTALLING WORDPRESS

Go to your web host website and log in to your AMP using the password you created at the end of Step 2.

Once logged in, do the following...

➤ Scroll down and click on the *Softaculous* icon.

Note: If you don't see the Softaculous icon, click on the cPanel icon and scroll down. You should see the Softaculous icon listed under software.

➤ Next click on the Wordpress icon and click install.

Go ahead and fill in the following information listed below, using Fig 3 as a guide...

- ➢ Software Setup
- ➢ Database Settings
- ➢ Site Settings
- ➢ Admin Account

Software Setup	
Choose Protocol:	Leave the protocol as http://. We will be installing a plugin that will change the protocol once SSL is enabled.
Choose Domain:	Choose the domain name that you registered in Step 1, to install Wordpress onto.
In Directory:	Leave this blank.
Database Name:	You can type one in if you like or just leave it as it is.
Database Settings	
Table Prefix:	The wp_ is the default prefix added to the database tables. You can leave it as it is or change it if you like.
Site Settings	
Site Name:	Type in your site name.
Site Description:	Type in a short tag line.
Enable Multisite:	You can leave this unchecked.
Admin Account	
Admin Username:	Type in your username. You will be using your username to log in to your Wordpress dashboard. **Do not** use ***admin*** as a username.
Admin Password:	Type in your password. Make it a strong one.
Admin Email:	Type in your admin email address. Make sure it's a valid email address. After Wordpress is installed, your admin info will be sent to this email address.

Figure 3

IMPORTANT EMAIL

After installation is complete you will receive an email that will contain your admin link, to log in to your Wordpress dashboard and the link to your website. Make sure you save and or write this information down.

WORDPRESS CONFIGURATIONS

Now let's do some wordpress configurations.

Go ahead and sign in to your wordpress dashboard. You can do this by clicking your wordpress admin url link that was sent to your admin email account or by typing in your wordpress admin url, (http://www.yourwebsite.com/wp-admin) in the address bar.

Scroll down the menu on the left hand side. Click on *Settings* and then *General* (Fig 3-1).

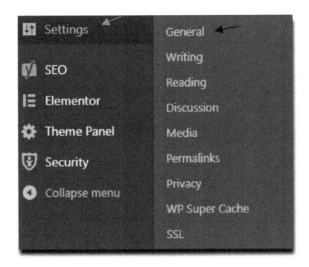

Figure 3-1

➤ Scroll down the page to set the correct time zone (**very important**) in your Wordpress dashboard. This is important because there is a configuration that can be done in iThemes Security that will allow you to lock your
Wordpress dashboard for a certain period of time. An example would be locking the Wordpress dashboard from, 10pm to 7am, while you're sleeping. With that in mind, the thing that you don't want to do, is accidently lock yourself out of your Wordpress dashboard, due to having the wrong time zone settings. *Please note that you do not have to configure this particular feature in the iTheme Security plugin.*

➢ After you set your time zone go ahead and pick your date and time format and click save changes.

Now let's configure the permalinks. Go back to the menu on the left hand side; under "*Settings*" click on "*Permalinks*" (Fig 3-2).

Figure 3-2

➢ Put a tick by "*post name*". Once you've done that, scroll down and click save changes.

Okay, the Wordpress configurations are done. Let's move on to installing a theme.

INSTALLING THEME

Scroll down the left hand side of your wordpress dashboard and hover over "*Appearance*" and then click on "*Themes*" (Fig 3-3).

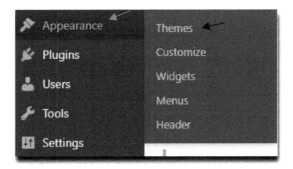

Figure 3-3

Once you're on the Themes page go to the top of the page and click the "*Add New*" button. Type OceanWP or GeneratePress in the search theme box (Fig 3-4). Both themes work great with the page builder plugin that will be used. Click the install button once you have decided on one of the themes.

Figure 3-4

After the installation is completed, click the blue activate button.

Now that the theme is active let's move on to the next step which is installing plugins.

Step 4

Page Builder and Plugins

Now that you have your *Content Management System* (Wordpress) installed and your theme installed and activated, it's time to download and install some plugins.

Let's move on to the fourth and final tool; which is a page builder plugin.

Plugins are just software components that add more functionality to a website.

PAGE BUILDER PLUGIN

The envelope is opened; and the winner is… The "Elementor Page Builder" plugin! The "Elementor Page Builder" is by far the easiest page builder, I have ever used. Guess what! It's also 100% free to use! Sometimes free is not always good but this free is.

There's a pro version of the Elementor Page Builder, which does cost and has even more bells and whistles to build professional looking websites. The good news is that you don't have to go all pro at this time to build a professional looking website because the free version of Elementor is more than enough to achieve that professional look that you want in a website! So you can put your credit card and or debit card away for now.

By using the Elementor Page Builder; there is no way, you can design a messed up looking website, unless, you've got your eyes closed. That's how easy, the Elementor Page Builder is, to use.

INSTALLING PLUGINS

Go to your wordpress dashboard and scroll down, hover over plugins and then click on *"Add New"* (Fig 4).

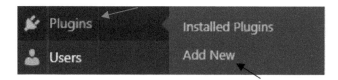

Figure 4

Type in *"Elementor Page Builder"* in the *"search plugin"* box (Fig 4-1).

Figure 4-1

The "Elementor Page Builder" plugin should be the first one listed. The author is "*Elementor.com*". Click on "*Install Now*"; after install, click on "*Activate*" *(Fig 4-2)*.

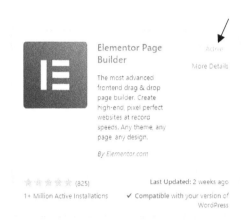

Figure 4-2

Please note that you have to activate each plugin after installation.

More Functionality

With those four basic reliable tools all set up and ready to go; additional plugins need to be downloaded and install to add more functionality to your wordpress website.

ADDING MORE FUNCTIONALITY

Below are 4 more plugins to install. These plugins will add some speed, security and search engine optimization (SEO) to your website.

Just follow the same steps you took when you installed the Elementor Page Builder plugin.

1. WP Super Cache- by Automatic
2. iThemes Security- by iThemes
3. Really Simple SSL- by Rogier Lankhorst (**Download this plugin but do not activate it yet. Activate this plugin after you have enable SSL in your cpanel**).
4. Yoast SEO- by Team Yoast

What do these plugins do?

o   The **WP Super Cache** plugin speeds up your website.

o   The **iThemes Security** plugin will add more security to your wordpress website. This is a plugin that you will have to configure yourself. There are some great YouTube videos on how to configure iThemes Security to protect your wordpress website.

o   The **Really Simple SSL** plugin will move your website to SSL. If you are, someone who is not familiar with code and configuring files, this plugin will take care of all that for you. *If you signed up with Inmotion Hosting click the "Manage Free Basic SSL" (Fig 5) icon and enable free SSL. Make sure you enable SSL before you activate the "The Really Simple SSL" plugin.*

Figure 5

- o The **Yoast** plugin will help with Search Engine Optimization. Just like the iThemes Security plugin, this plugin requires some configuration. Once again there are some great YouTube videos on how to configure the Yoast SEO plugin to get the best SEO results.

Getting Clear

If the "4 Tools To Use To Build A Website Easily & Effortlessly", were not clear, as you were going along.

They are...

1. NameCheap
2. Inmotion Hosting
3. Wordpress
4. Elementor Page Builder

These 4 reliable tools will get you going designing and building websites with ease!

That's It

Now that you know of, four reliable tools, when will you start your build? It took me many years but that doesn't have to be you!

And that my friend is it! That wasn't so bad! Right?

Lessons Learned

Here are a couple of lessons, I learned, the hard way, when I first started out.

Lesson number one was.... Not doing enough research, on a web host services.

Here's a little story about a web host, I used, in the past.

This is why I listed number four (Malware Protection) as a must have service, in a web host.

One of my websites that I built was shut down by the web host because they scanned the website and said that they found malware on the site. I was new to web design and didn't know that web host could just take someone's website down. Now, I'm not saying that this wasn't listed in the terms and agreement. It is possible that I could've over looked that term and agreement.

In the email that they sent they stated that the website would not be enable until all the malware was removed. I didn't even know what malware looked like. So I had no clue what to look for.

So I started to do some research on how to remove malware and ended up coming across a bunch of articles written on this particular web host who would disable customers websites because of malware they claimed they found on their(meaning the customer) website. Some people even stated that this web host would say that there was malware on their site, even if, there was none. This particular web host would then recommend a company *'that they were affiliated with'* to remove the malware. Of course this came with a price.

Now that I was in the know, I definitely didn't want to experience this again. I cancelled my services with them and begin to look for a web host that offered free malware protection. I was under the impression that all web host protected their servers from malware. I didn't know it was individualized by websites; if that is even true. ***Lesson Learned***!

Lesson number two was..... I registered my domain name with that same web host that I talked about earlier and when I cancelled my service with that web host; I didn't even think about the domain name I had registered for free. When I finally decided on a new web host, I knew that I had to point the domain name, to the new web host nameservers. But wait, how would I do that? Who did the domain name belong to? I did a search on the domain name and of course it had "Make Offer" beside the domain name. I clicked the *"Make Offer"* button out of curiosity and saw that I would have to pay $199.00 or higher to use this domain name again.

Again this could have been a term and agreement, I missed; about who owns the domain name that was registered for free, if services are cancelled. ***Lesson Learned***!

Quiz Answers

Quiz Me 1

1. c

2. False

3. False

Quiz Me 2

1. b

2. False

3. False

Conclusion

Thank you for taking the time to read "4 Tools To Use To Build A Website Easily & Effortlessly". I hope this book has helped you.

My goal with this book was to make it a quick read and at the same time provide great value.

Thanks again and enjoy your day!

When I believe in myself I AM GOD in action!

Rev. Ike

4 TOOLS TO USE TO BUILD A WEBSITE
Easily & Effortlessly

4 TOOLS TO USE TO BUILD A WEBSITE
Easily & Effortlessly

4 TOOLS TO USE TO BUILD A WEBSITE
Easily & Effortlessly

www.ingramcontent.com/pod-product-compliance
Lightning Source LLC
Chambersburg PA
CBHW070902070326
40690CB00009B/1962